D0576461

Book 29—Paul

The First Missionaries

Written by Anne de Graaf

Illustrated by José Pérez Montero

Family Time Bible Stories

Standard Publishing

PAUL—THE FIRST MISSIONARIES

1 and 2 Corinthians; Acts 20—28; Romans; Ephesians; Philippians; Colossians

About Paul's Letters to the Corinthians, Romans, Philippians, Ephesians and Colossians

These stories describe the amazing life and times of Paul. As he spread the Good News from one land to the next, he became one of the greatest Christian leaders ever. This was quite a miracle since Paul used to be a man who wanted very much to hurt the Christians.

Paul wrote two letters to the church in Corinth. It was an evil city during Paul's time and Christians living there had more than their share of difficulties. The first letter is an example of how real the fight to follow Jesus can be. The second letter was probably written about a year after the first. Paul heard that the Corinthian Christians managed to solve their problems and are again trying their hardest to follow Jesus.

As Paul and his team of missionaries go from one city to the next, they built up the churches, encouraging, teaching, and leading the new Christians. Paul had always wanted to visit Rome. It was the capital of the Roman empire. This covered all of Europe, including Britain and parts of the Middle East. But the Christians in Rome faced a terrible danger. Their city was the home of the emperor. Paul strengthened the church there by reminding them of God's free forgiveness and offer of new life.

Paul was finally put in prison by his enemies. Years went by as he stood trial over and over again for no crime at all. In prison, he wrote letters to the Philippians, Ephesians and Colossians, urging them all to stand strong in their faith in Jesus. Eventually Paul appealed to the emperor. Since he was a Roman citizen, this meant he would be taken to Rome.

Paul spent at least two years in Rome teaching and preaching to everyone who visited him. How Paul's life ended is unknown. Many people believe he died in Rome around A.D. 67. But the work he began and the letters he wrote will go on inspiring Christians forever.

CORINTH
The City With Problems

1 Corinthians 1:1—9:27

While Paul was in Ephesus, he continued writing his friends in the other cities he had visited. Paul was especially worried about the Corinthians. Theirs was a city filled with people who did many wrong things. It was very hard for the Christians there to remember how to follow Jesus.

While Paul was staying in Ephesus, he heard that things were not going well for the Corinthian Christians. He was worried about them. They seemed to be fighting each other, instead of working together. He wrote this first letter to remind them of what is really important.

He warned them not to cheat each other, or decide what is right and wrong the way the non-Christians did.

Paul also wrote that if two Christians had a disagreement, they should not go before a public court. "Surely there is a wise man among you who can settle your problems."

Paul gave the Corinthians advice about marriage. Men and women who marry should know ahead of time that it takes the blessing of God and hard work to make any marriage work.

Paul also warned the Corinthians not to do anything that would cause another Christian to do wrong.

Paul was an apostle of Jesus. He did everything he could to tell all people the Good News about Jesus.

True Love

1 Corinthians 10:1—13:13

Paul's first letter to the Corinthians was full of useful advice.

He wrote about the Lord's Supper. It is a time to remember the Lord's death and what it means. It is also a time when Christians remember that they all belong to one family, the body of Christ.

Many of the believers in Corinth were not thinking about Jesus during the Lord's Supper. Paul told them to eat the bread and drink the cup to show others about the Lord's death until He returns.

Paul also wrote that all the people who believe in Jesus make up one family of Christ. Some people are the arms or legs, others are the eyes, others

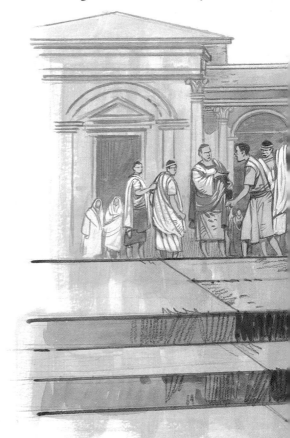

are the ears. Alone, they cannot do much, but together they can do God's work on earth. Christians are the eyes, hands and feet of Jesus, all working together like a team.

Paul wrote to the Corinthians about love. Nowhere else is there such a list of what love really means.

"Love is patient, love is kind. If you love someone, don't be jealous, don't brag or act stuck up. Don't always try to get your own way, getting angry easily. Don't be happy with evil, but look for the truth. Real love lasts forever."

TAKING CARE OF OTHERS
Eutychus Falls Out the Window

Acts 20:1-12; 1 Corinthians 16:1-11

While Paul was in Ephesus, he heard that the people in Jerusalem were going hungry. There wasn't enough food to go around. Paul believed that if the Christians in Jerusalem were hungry, Christians everywhere should try to help them.

Paul wrote to the Corinthians asking them to save whatever money they could for the Jerusalem Christians. "Once a week, put something aside. Then when I arrive, there will be enough for me to take to Jerusalem."

After the riot in Ephesus, Paul left the city to collect money from the other churches. Paul visited one church after another. He did more than collect

money. He preached and taught and God worked miracles through him.

In Troas, Paul met with the believers. He taught until very late at night because he planned to leave the next day. The meeting place was an upstairs room and there were many lamps in the room.

A young man named Eutychus was sitting in the window. As Paul taught, Eutychus began to feel sleepy. Finally, he went sound asleep and fell right out the window!

His friends ran down three flights of stairs to pick up the young man. He was dead! Then Paul went down to look at Eutychus. "Don't worry!" he told the others as he hugged him. "He's alive!" Then they all went upstairs again and ate. They listened to Paul's teaching until sunrise.

When Paul finally left, the others took Eutychus home. They probably laughed and shook their heads in wonder that he was alive again.

Good News From Corinth

2 Corinthians 1:8—6:10

While Paul was in Troas, he waited for news

about the church in Corinth.

Titus was supposed to bring this news, but Paul could not find Titus. So Paul left Troas and went to Macedonia.

There, Paul heard from Titus. He told Paul that the Corinthians were trying hard to do all that Paul had taught them. Paul was so happy, he wrote them another letter. He told them how glad he was to hear things were going better for the Christians in Corinth. He told them about all his travels.

"We don't ever get tired of working for Jesus," Paul wrote. He encouraged the Corinthians, telling them to think about being with Jesus in Heaven. "We have small problems on earth, but they won't last. Then God will give us a home in Heaven that will last forever."

Paul told the Corinthians, "More than anything else, we want to please God. We are servants of God, no matter what happens. We have many problems. We are beaten and thrown in prison. We work hard and sometimes get no food. But we show we love God by living right, telling the truth, and being kind to others. God's power helps us."

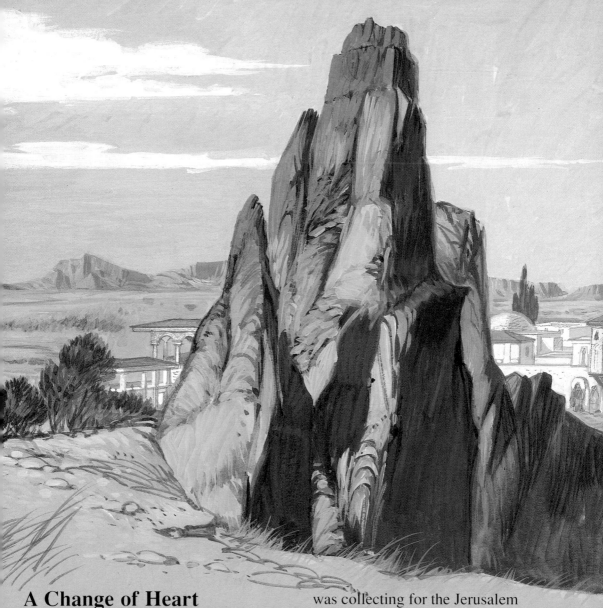

A Change of Heart

2 Corinthians 6:11—11:33

After Paul had shared with the Corinthians what he had been learning lately, he talked to them about the good news Titus had brought him.

Titus told Paul that the Corinthians had changed their hearts and lives. They had started doing what God wanted them to do. Paul was so happy!

Then Paul reported on the money he was collecting for the Jerusalem church. The churches in Macedonia had given much, even though they were very poor. These were the same churches where people had been beaten and killed for being followers of Jesus. It probably wasn't easy for them to give, yet they had done so willingly. "God loves the person who gives happily."

Paul warned the Corinthians not to listen to everyone who preached to them. "Someone might tell you to follow a different person than the One we preached. Follow only Jesus."

Paul described the problems he had gone through because he preached the Good News. Paul was brave for Jesus.

How Paul Sees Himself

Romans 1:1; 2 Corinthians 12:1—13:14

Through Paul's letters, we can see what kind of man Paul was. Before he became a Christian, he had been a proud man, proud of how he hurt the Christians. Then Jesus had made Paul take a hard and painful look at himself. Paul went from the Christians' worst enemy to one of their most dedicated leaders.

Yet he did not see himself as great. Just the opposite, he saw himself as weak. There was something that bothered Paul. We don't know what it was, but it was a painful problem.

Paul learned that being weak was not bad. God can help the weak people since they will ask for His help. God cannot use people who think they can do everything.

Paul even called himself a slave and servant of God. Like Jesus, he taught about the importance of serving others. Paul did not think much of himself as a man. He was not proud of being clever or of having gone to the best schools. The only thing that mattered to Paul was what God thought of him.

A LETTER TO ROME

The Good News

Romans 1:2—8:39

Not long after Paul wrote the Corinthians, he was able to visit them. It was a happy day when Paul entered Corinth and saw for himself that the problems had been worked out. He also collected the last of the money which would be sent to Jerusalem to help the Christians there.

While Paul was staying with his friends in Corinth, he wrote a letter to the Christians in Rome. Paul had never been to Rome, but he wanted very much to go there. At that time the Roman empire ruled all over Europe, most of the Middle East, and North Africa. Rome was the center of it all. There was a group of believers in Rome and Paul wanted to meet them.

In his letter to the Romans, Paul wrote about what it means to become a Christian. "We have all done wrong things. We are made right with God through faith in Jesus." Paul also explained God's plans for the world and for the Jews.

When Paul wrote this letter, he had thought he would soon see the Christians in Rome. Little did he know it would be three years before he reached Rome. In the meantime this letter taught them, as it does us, about Jesus' Good News.

Paul wrote about Abraham and what a special man he was. Abraham trusted God, no matter what happened. That's what Christians should do as well.

"No matter where we go, no matter what happens to us, no matter if we live or die, there's nothing that can ever separate us from the love of God. This love is ours through Jesus."

How to Live

Romans 12:1—16:27

Paul had spent many years starting churches and teaching people about Jesus. In his letter to the Christians in Rome, he talked about the things Jesus taught and how to live as a follower of Jesus.

He told them not to

become like the people of this world, but to do what is good and pleasing to God. Paul said, "Work hard. Share with other people. Do not be too proud. Obey the laws and respect the leaders who are in charge."

Paul wrote about how to make hard decisions. Christians should try to make peace and do what will help one another.

As in many of his letters, Paul wrote about his travels and the churches he had visited. Paul ended his letter to the Romans by saying he would see them soon. He would take the money to Jerusalem first and try to visit Rome on his way to Spain.

Finally, Paul sent greetings to all the people he had met who now lived in Rome.

A ROUNDABOUT WAY TO ROME

A Warning for Ephesus

Acts 20:17-38

While Paul was on his way to Jerusalem, he tried to stop to teach in as many places as possible. Many of the churches in the different towns were groups of people who first heard about Jesus from Paul himself. Many years had gone by since Paul first started preaching. Now, as he headed for Jerusalem with the money he had collected, he wanted to say good-bye to some of these old friends.

He had decided not to stop at Ephesus, because he wanted to hurry to Jerusalem. But in Miletus, he sent a message to the leaders of the church at Ephesus asking them to meet him at the port where his boat would be docked, ready to sail.

The old friends talked about the early years, the hard times, and the good times. "You know I always served God," Paul said to them. "I must finish the work God wants me to do. I must go to Jerusalem, and I don't know what will happen."

Paul had many enemies. In every city where he had preached, there were people who wanted to kill him. Paul knew that more problems and even jail waited for him in Jerusalem.

Paul warned his friends from Ephesus that they should be on the alert and take good care of each other.

When he could no longer put off leaving, Paul knelt down and prayed with them all. They cried and hugged Paul. Together they all walked down to the ship that was waiting to take Paul away.

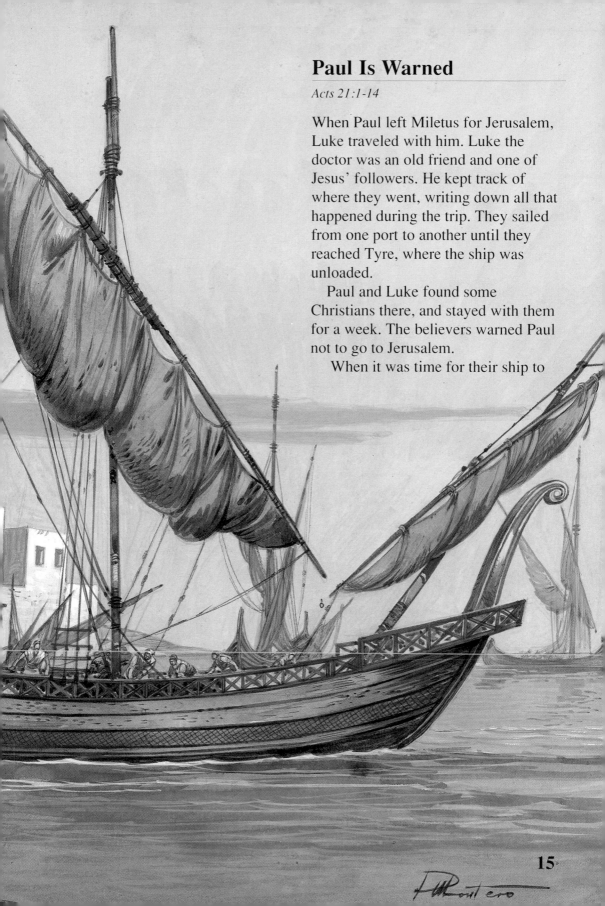

Paul Is Warned

Acts 21:1-14

When Paul left Miletus for Jerusalem,
Luke traveled with him. Luke the
doctor was an old friend and one of
Jesus' followers. He kept track of
where they went, writing down all that
happened during the trip. They sailed
from one port to another until they
reached Tyre, where the ship was
unloaded.

Paul and Luke found some
Christians there, and stayed with them
for a week. The believers warned Paul
not to go to Jerusalem.

When it was time for their ship to

16

sail again, all the believers and their families came down to the beach to pray together. They knelt on the sand and said good-bye.

From Tyre, Paul and Luke went to Ptolemais. They stayed one day visiting with believers there.

Then they traveled to Caesarea. Paul and Luke stayed with Philip. After several days, a prophet named Agabus came to Paul and showed him how terrible it was going to be in Jerusalem. Agabus took his belt and tied up his hands and feet. "This is how the Jews in Jerusalem will tie you up and hand you over to the Romans."

When the other believers heard this, they begged Paul not to go to Jerusalem. But Paul said, "I am ready to be tied up. I am ready to die for Jesus."

When the others saw that they could not change Paul's mind, they said, "We will pray that what God wants will happen."

Taken Prisoner in Jerusalem

Acts 21:15-36

Philip's house had been the last stop before Jerusalem. Some of the believers from there joined Paul and Luke on the last leg of their journey. The Christians in Jerusalem welcomed Paul and his friends. He met with James, the brother of Jesus and one of the leaders of the church in Jerusalem. Together with the other leaders, Paul talked about what was happening in the other churches. They all thanked God.

Then the church leaders warned Paul that, as always, there were plenty of Jews who did not like what Paul was doing.
"Go to the temple and pray. Offer sacrifices. Then no one can complain about you," his friends advised Paul. So for several days Paul did this, keeping the Jewish Law so no one could accuse him of doing anything wrong.

But it did not help. He had been in Jerusalem only a week when some of the Jewish leaders, his old enemies saw him and caused a riot. "This is the man who preaches against the Jews! He has broken our laws!" the men screamed. They dragged him out of the temple and tried to kill him. Just in time, the commander of the Roman army in Jerusalem heard about the riot and brought soldiers to rescue Paul. The crowd stopped beating Paul. The commander asked, "Who is

this man? What did he do?" Some people shouted one thing and some another.

Because of all the confusion and shouting, the commander decided to take Paul to safety. His soldiers had to carry Paul so the crowd wouldn't grab him and hurt him. "Kill him!" they shouted.

On Trial

Acts 21:37—23:11

When the Roman soldiers took Paul away, they did not know who he was or what he had done wrong. They thought he was a criminal from Egypt. But Paul spoke to them in Greek, "Please, let me speak to the crowd," he said. The commander agreed.

Paul stood up in front of the crowd and motioned for them to be quiet. He told them who he was, how Jesus had changed him from an enemy of the Christians to one of their leaders. He told how God had sent him to preach to Jewish people and non-Jewish people.

When the crowd heard this, they stopped listening and started yelling, "Away with him! He should not be allowed to live!" The commander ordered the soldiers to take Paul inside the building and beat him.

"Wait a minute!" Paul warned a soldier. "Are you allowed to beat a Roman citizen without a fair trial?" The commander could get into a lot of trouble if Paul was hurt without a good reason. So the commander ordered the Jewish leaders in the crowd to meet to accuse Paul.

The next day, Paul stood in front of the Jewish leaders. They did not want to listen to him. Before Paul had said very much, the leaders were fighting one another. One group was for Paul, the other was against him.

The commander was afraid the Jewish leaders would hurt Paul, so he ordered the soldiers to take him to the army building.

The next night, while Paul was in prison, the Lord stood next to him. He said, "Be brave, Paul. Just as you told the people here in Jerusalem about me, so you must tell them in Rome."

Under Roman Guard

Acts 23:12—24:27

After the riot, some of the Jewish leaders met and made a plan to kill Paul. More than forty of them promised, "We won't eat or drink anything until we have killed Paul." They went to the other religious leaders and said, "We have plotted how to kill Paul. You tell the commander to bring him to you so you can ask him more questions. We will be waiting to attack him while he is on his way here."

But Paul's nephew overheard their plans and told Paul. Paul had the boy tell the Roman commander what he had heard. The commander knew he must protect Paul and make sure he got a fair trial. So the Roman captain came up with a plan of his own.

He called two hundred soldiers, seventy horsemen and two hundred soldiers with spears. Then, in the middle of the night, they smuggled

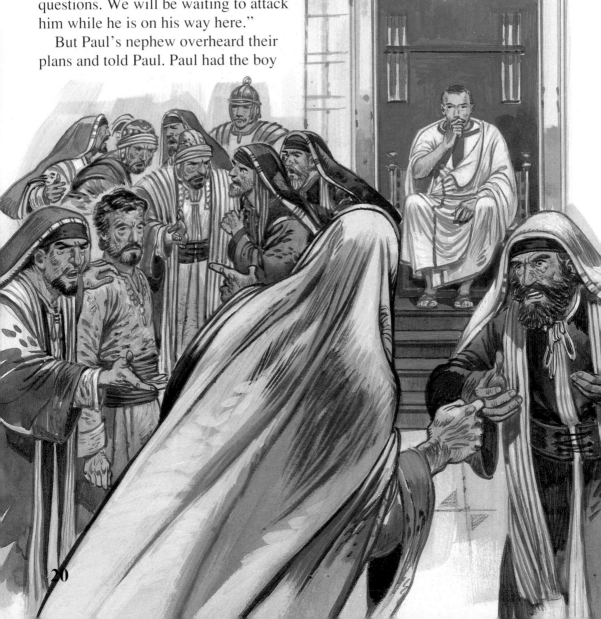

Paul out of the city and brought him to
Caesarea. That was where the
governor, Felix, lived.

Paul defended himself before Felix.
Felix already knew much about what
the Christians believed. After hearing
Paul, he said he would decide the case
later. Felix ordered an officer to keep
Paul guarded, but Paul was allowed
some freedom. His friends could come
and bring him things he needed.

Several days later, Felix and his
Jewish wife, Drusilla, asked to see
Paul. Felix listened to Paul again as he
told him about believing in Jesus. Then
Paul spoke about living right. He also
told about a time when God would
judge the world.

Felix said, "That's enough for now.
Go away. I will call for you later when
I have more time." Felix had hoped
Paul would give him money to let him
go. Felix often sent for Paul to talk with
him.

Felix kept Paul in prison to please
the Jews. After two years, Festus
replaced Felix as governor.

Paul Must Die!

Acts 25:1—26:32

As a Roman citizen, Paul was supposed
to get a fair trial. Instead he had spent
two years in prison. When Felix was
replaced by Festus, things did not get
any better for Paul.

Three days after Festus became
governor, he went to Jerusalem. He met
with the Jewish leaders to hear their
side of the story. They said, "Bring
Paul back to Jerusalem." They were

plotting to kill Paul on his way to Jerusalem. Festus said, "No. Paul will stay in Caesarea. Some of you can go with me and accuse him there." They went and accused Paul of one crime after another. But no one had any proof. Finally, Festus, who did not want to get into trouble, asked Paul, "Are you willing to go to Jerusalem to go on trial?"

Paul said, "I'm on trial here. You're the governor. I should be judged here. If I have done nothing wrong, you can't hand me over to these men. I want Caesar to hear me."

Festus had no choice but to make sure Paul went to Rome and was tried by the emperor. But before he let Paul go, Festus asked King Agrippa what he thought of the case.

Once again, Paul told what happened, this time in front of King Agrippa and many other important people. When he finished, Agrippa said to him, "Do you think you can convince me to become a Christian so easily?" Then he turned to Festus. "This man could go free, but he has asked to go before Caesar. He must go to Rome."

Shipwrecked!

Acts 27:1-26

Paul was finally on his way to Rome. But instead of traveling as a free man, on his way to visit friends, Paul was a prisoner.

The soldier in charge of Paul was an officer named Julius. He could see that Paul was not dangerous, and treated

him kindly. Luke and another of Paul's friends were allowed to travel with him.

They changed ships, going from port to port. Over and over again they ran into bad weather. Finally the storms made sailing almost impossible. The ship carrying Paul found a harbor on

the island of Crete. Paul warned them, "If we don't stop here for the winter, we'll lose the cargo, and perhaps our lives." But the owner of the ship did not agree. He did not listen to Paul and they sailed on.

Soon a very strong wind caught the ship and there was nothing the crew could do. The storm tossed the ship and waves swamped its decks. The crew threw the cargo overboard. For many days it was so dark, no one could see the sun or stars. They all thought they would die!

Then Paul stood up. "Men, you should have listened to me. But be brave. No one will die. Last night an angel from God told me I would stand before Caesar. Your lives will be saved. But we will land on an island somewhere."

Safe in Malta

Acts 27:27-29, 33—28:10

The storm raged for two weeks. For most of that time, the people on board had not eaten much. They just waited. Finally, they thought they were getting close to an island.

It was night and the sailors were afraid the ship would crash on the rocks. So they dropped four anchors.

Some of the sailors tried to secretly escape from the ship by lowering the lifeboat into the sea. They wanted the others to think they were dropping more anchors. Paul told the soldiers, "Don't let them go overboard. Unless these men stay on the ship, you cannot be saved!" So the soldiers cut the ropes that held the lifeboat and let it fall away.

Just before the sun came up, Paul asked all the people to eat something. "You need to eat to stay alive." Then he thanked God for what little food they still had, and all two hundred and seventy-six people ate. When the sun came up that morning and they could see the island, they tried to bring the ship closer.

The ship hit sand and got stuck. The waves pounded against the wood and the ship started breaking up. The soldiers wanted to kill the prisoners to keep them from escaping. But Julius

would not let them kill anyone. He ordered those who could swim to jump overboard and swim for shore. The rest used pieces of the ship or boards.

Once on shore, they found out the island was Malta, close to Italy. Luke wrote that the people who lived there were very kind to them. They built a fire for the wet and tired sailors. Then they helped the men eat. During the meal, Paul was bitten by a poisonous snake. The people from the island

thought to themselves, "Ah, this must be a very bad man." But when nothing happened to Paul's arm, they thought, "This man must be a god!"

They brought Paul to one of the leaders whose father was sick. Paul prayed, laid hands on him, and healed him. After this, many of the people of Malta brought their sick friends and family to Paul.

When the group left the island people gave them gifts and supplies for the rest of the trip to Rome.

Rome!

Acts 28:11-31

About three years after Paul wrote his friends in Rome that he would like to visit, he arrived. Believers from Rome came to meet Paul, Luke, and the others while they were still far from the city. When Paul saw them, he thanked God and felt brave again.

The Romans did not put Paul in prison this time. They let him live by himself with a soldier to guard him. Paul talked to the Jewish leaders in Rome and told them what had happened in Jerusalem. They said, "We haven't heard anything about you. We would like to hear what you have to say."

Paul and the Jewish leaders met later to talk. Paul told them about the kingdom of God. He tried to convince them to believe in Jesus. He used the writings of Moses and the prophets to help persuade them.

Some of the Jewish leaders believed, but some did not. They argued about

what Paul had said.

Paul said one more thing to them. "I want you to know that God has offered the non-Jewish people His salvation. They will listen."

Paul stayed in Rome two years. He welcomed visitors and taught them the Good News of Jesus. No one tried to stop him from preaching.

WE ARE ONE
God's Plan for People

Ephesians 1:1—6:24

While Paul was in prison, he wrote several letters to his friends, believers in the churches he had started.

At that time, there were still problems between non-Jewish Christians and Jewish Christians. One group thought they were better than the other. Paul wrote to the church in Ephesus that they should try to understand what God wants, and pray for more love in their hearts.

"Jesus made both Jews and non-Jews one family. The Good News about Jesus brings all people together." Paul wrote that Jesus made it possible for everyone to belong to God's family.

Paul prayed that the Ephesians would understand how wide, how long, how high, and how deep Christ's love is. He told them how God's people should live. "Be patient and love each other. Live together in peace. Work together to make the church grow."

Paul also wrote the Ephesians about the best way to live in a family. "Wives, respect your husbands. Husbands, love your wives as Christ loved the church. Children, do what your parents tell you. Parents, don't make your children angry, but teach them about the Lord."

Paul encouraged the Christians to work hard. "Remember to work as if you were working for God."

New Life in Christ

Colossians 1:1—4:18

Another letter Paul wrote while he was in prison was to his friends in Colossae. This was a small town fairly close to Ephesus. There were several small groups of Christians in that area.

Paul heard reports that the Colossians were not putting Jesus first in their lives. They had forgotten what Jesus had done. Paul reminded them who Jesus is and told them to put first things first. "You used to be separated from God. Christ has made you God's friends."

Paul gave them practical advice, too. "Get rid of these: anger, doing things to hurt others, bad language, and lying. Do these instead: Be kind and patient, forgive each other, and love each other."

Again, Paul taught about families, asking wives and husbands to work together, to make Jesus the leader of the home.

Lastly, he sent greetings to all his old friends. "Make the most of your chances to tell others about Jesus. Be sure to pray. Pray for us too, that we might be able to tell more people about the Good News."

Happy in the Lord

Philippians 1:1—4:23

When Paul wrote his friends in Philippi, he knew he soon might be sentenced to death. Timothy was with him, as well as Epaphroditus. These two men must have been a great comfort to Paul.

Paul wrote about his prayers for them. "I pray that your love will grow even more and that you will come to know Jesus better and better."

Paul used his letter to let them know that people were still hearing about Jesus. "All the palace guards and everyone else knows I am a believer in Christ. The Christians here are much braver now about telling others the Good News."

He told them to work together to spread the Good News. "Make me happy by having the same mind and purpose. Think and act like Jesus."

Paul wrote that knowing Jesus was more important than anything else in life.

He encouraged the Philippians to continue following the Lord. "Be happy in the Lord always. Don't worry about anything. Instead, pray and thank God. Think about things that are true and right and good. Do what I told you, and God will be with you."

Paul wrote that he was happy in the Lord. "I have learned to be happy any time and in everything that happens. I can do all things because of Christ who gives me the strength."

Paul sent greetings from the believers with him. "God will give you everything you need."

Old Testament